Bloomsbury Collection of Modern Art

Cézanne and the Post-Impressionists

BLOOMSBURY BOOKS
LONDON

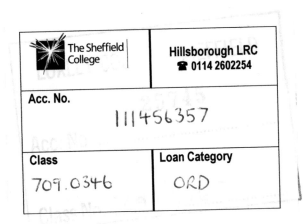
Copyright 1970 on the original series *Mensili d'Arte* by Gruppo Editoriale Fabbri S.p.A., Milan

This edition published 1989 by Bloomsbury Books
an imprint of Godfrey Cave Associates Limited
42 Bloomsbury Street, London WC1B 3QJ

ISBN 1 870630 12 2

Printed in Italy by Gruppo Editoriale Fabbri, S.p.A., Milan

© by S.I.A.E. 1970/1989 for the works of Emile Bernard, Maximilien Luce

Around 1880 the revolutionary art movement called Impressionism had reached its peak. Already, however, dissensions and dissatisfactions were apparent among the members of the group. Their former preoccupation with naturalism and with the effects of light and atmosphere no longer seemed adequate. The group separated, each artist following his own independent path.

It was not that the Impressionists repudiated their earlier color discoveries, but—for many of them—that they now wanted to apply these in a more substantial way. The evanescent shimmer of light was no longer enough. They wanted that light to envelop and define solid form rather than to dissolve it.

Nor were these artists content any longer with their rather passive role of a perceiving eye. ("Monet is just an eye," Cézanne had said, "but what an eye!") They felt that the perceiving eye should be controlled by the conceiving intellect, that art should have a deeper and more permanent significance than that afforded by a mere "impression." The spontaneous effect that had been their aim had been achieved by their passive acceptance of a subject as it was presented to them, natural and unarranged. Now this effect seemed to them merely haphazard. They set out, each in his own way, to reorganize nature.

Seurat and Neo-Impressionism

One artist, Georges Seurat, developed a kind of rational, "scientific" Impressionism as opposed to the more intuitive Impressionism of his predecessors. He believed that Impressionist ideas could be condensed into a completely scientific system and that he could construct his paintings according to precise rules. He had rules for everything. "The little green chemist," Gauguin called him. In Seurat's opinion color could be handled with all the exactitude and significance of mathematics or music. He analyzed its emotional value, too, systematizing it as color, tone, and line. Joy, for instance, glory, gaiety, and love were warm colors—yellow, orange, and red—in brilliant tones and upward-surging lines. Conversely, sadness, death, failure would be conveyed by cold colors, dark tones, and downward-slanting lines.

Seurat applied his paint in tiny dots of pure color in an optical mixture, rather like the dots in color lithography. His friend Paul Signac defined it as "a method of securing the utmost luminosity, color, and harmony by the use of all the colors of the spectrum and all degrees of those colors without any mixing." His method came to be called Neo-Impressionism, Pointillism, or Divisionism. With remarkable precision, following the rules he set out, he created canvases having all the luminosity of pure Impressionism, but with a solidity of form that was new.

Seurat died at thirty-one. Because of the shortness of his life and because of the intricacy of his method he painted only six large-scale canvases (though a number of smaller ones). The first of these was *Bathing at Asnières* (Plate 14). For this he made many preparatory sketches in which he reduced all the forms to basic geometric shapes, and posed and arranged the figures in careful balance. Nothing was left to chance.

The composition lends itself to fascinating analysis in its play of curves and diagonals. For instance, the curve that defines the stomach of the boy cupping his hands is repeated in the right shoulder of the swimming boy and of the boy seated on the bank, and in the straw hat, and the haunch of the dog. Diagonals make a similar repeated pattern: the man's recumbent figure, the careful disarray of clothing on the grass, the leg, arm, and shadow of the more distant figure, the line of the river bank. The curves and diagonals are used like musical motifs in such interesting relationships and with such imagination and humor that their repetition is never monotonous.

And whereas Impressionist painters had tended to dissolve contours, Seurat's figures are clearly outlined by contrasts of dark and light that place them firmly in space. There is a solidity to them, almost a timelessness, that is very different from the swift, fleeting quality of Impressionism.

Bathing at Asnières was exhibited in the first Show of Independent Artists in 1884. This show was organized by the artists whose work was regularly rejected by the conservative annual Salon. These artists represented the latest movements in the Paris art world, such as Seurat's Divisionism. Not only did they organize

an annual show to give an opportunity to innovative artists, who might otherwise have found it impossible to exhibit their works, but later in 1884 they formed the Society of Independent Artists to further their aims. Whereas the Salon's jury sifted out any artist who did not conform to its criteria of traditional themes and academic style, and the Impressionists restricted their shows to works by members of the group and invited friends, the Independents welcomed all artists, whatever their theories.

Two years later occurred the second Show of the Independents and the eighth and final Impressionist Show (which by this time had dropped the word "Impressionist" from its name, as no longer applicable, and was called simply an "Exhibition of Painting"). At both of these shows Seurat exhibited his masterpiece, *A Sunday Afternoon on the Island of La Grande-Jatte* (Plate 17). Today critics consider that, if Seurat had painted only this one picture, he would still be considered one of the finest artists of modern times. But in 1886 when it was first exhibited one critic wrote: "Strip his figures of the colored fleas that cover them, and underneath you will find nothing, no thought, no soul."

The picture is a large one, seven by ten feet, and Seurat spent two years completing it. In spite of the almost excessive care with which it is composed, in spite of the complete motionlessness of the figures, which have all the animation of dressmakers' dummies, still the scene has tremendous sparkle and vitality. The figures are at once doll-like and human. They are reduced to basic, idealized forms and yet they have individual personality. They are drawn with solemnity, but also with gentle humor. They have a classic timelessness and yet are as expressive of contemporary French life as any of the figures of Renoir.

Humor in serious painting is a comparative rarity. Seurat's is subtle, quiet, genial, completely free of mockery or cynicism. There is no caricature about the figures of *La Grande-Jatte*. They are drawn with affectionate good humor. We feel Seurat's tenderness for the little girl in the center of the picture, walking so sedately beside her mother, prim and grown-up in her best white dress: We are aware of the live little body under the artist's simplification. We sense his tolerant amusement at the self-importance of the couple in the right foreground who have obviously come for the pleasure of being seen in their Sunday finery. Their self-consciousness contrasts with the complete unself-consciousness of the dapper gentleman practicing on his trumpet in the background and the relaxed pipe smoker in the left foreground.

A number of artists, among them Paul Signac, imitated Seurat's method. But they were artists of lesser stature. Seurat's method without his genius produced results that were not notable, a fact which would have come as a surprise to

SEURAT *Portrait of Edmond François Aman-Jean* (62.2 x 47.6 cm) New York, Metropolitan Museum of Art

SIGNAC *Passage du Puits Bertin, Clichy* (24.3 x 36.5 cm) New York, Metropolitan Museum of Art

4

him, for he had always considered the science of his system to be exclusively responsible for his achievement: "They see poetry in what I have done. No, I apply my method, and that is all there is to it."

Seurat's desire to restore solidity and architectural order to Impressionist painting was shared by Cézanne. "My aim," he said, "was to make Impressionism into something solid and enduring like the art of the museums." But the way he set out to achieve his aim was entirely new.

Cézanne

Perhaps no artist ever brought to his art less natural talent and facility than Cézanne. The guilds and workshops of any earlier period would certainly have rejected him. He struggled all his life to develop the technical competence to express on canvas what he experienced when confronted by nature. This struggle was not made easier by his contradictory nature, at once inhibited and tempestuous.

Cézanne was a native of Aix-en-Provence, in southern France. He was an incorrigible provincial, never able to feel at home in Paris. His manners were boorish, sometimes intentionally so in order to cover up his awkwardness.

Pissarro became like a father to him. "Pissarro could teach even a stone to draw correctly," the American Impressionist painter, Mary Cassatt, once said. Until he joined the older master at Auvers-sur-Oise, Cézanne had almost never worked outdoors, directly from his subject, but had painted turgidly dramatic pictures from his imagination. His colors were dark and gloomy and his paint was laid on as if with a trowel. Under Pissarro's influence he changed his subject matter, limited himself to three basic colors and their direct variants, lightened his colors, and thinned his pigment. But the latter remained thick enough so that one critic, after the first Impressionist Show of 1874, called Cézanne the "pistol painter," implying that he fired paint at his canvas from a gun. One of the three paintings Cézanne exhibited at this show was *The House of the Hanged Man, Auvers* (Plate 1), which plainly shows Pissarro's influence.

After the show of 1877 Cézanne never again exhibited with the Impressionists, but isolated himself at Aix. For almost twenty years he did not exhibit at all, except for the few pictures that were hung in Père Tanguy's little artists' supply shop in Paris. *Zola's House at Médan* (Plate 3) is perhaps the most Impressionist painting he ever made, but still his interest is plainly in solidity of form rather than atmospheric effect.

Cézanne's revolutionary artistic discovery, which had been hinted at but not fully realized by Seurat, was that color might be used instead of modeling to achieve form. With Cézanne color *is* form. Each dab of paint takes, in relation to every other dab, a certain definite, predetermined position in space. The irregular planes established by these particles of color create the forms of objects and locate them with regard to each other and the picture plane. But at the same time that he was establishing objects in space, he limited the space to preserve the unity of his two-dimensional canvas. He did not want his canvas to be a hole through which the viewer peered into deep space, like some Renaissance painting in which a wall or ceiling seems to disappear. He wanted to keep the surface of his canvas flat, and yet stimulate the viewer to the same experience of form and color that the subject had inspired in him.

To accomplish this was a lifelong struggle. But the struggle resulted in innovations whose impact on succeeding artists was so great that Cézanne has come to be known as the "Father of Modern Art." He himself was aware of the originality of his inventions—"I am the primitive of a new art," he said—though he could not, of course, have had any idea of the scope of his influence on the art of the twentieth century.

In his later paintings Cézanne reduced his subject matter to basic geometric shapes, the cube, the cone, the sphere, the cylinder, whether that subject was a woman with a coffeepot (Plate 6) or a landscape of trees and rocks (Plate 5). This facet of his art was to form the basis, some twenty years later, for the new Cubist movement. But in spite of the fact that his skeletal forms look like a kind of shorthand for reality, they impress themselves on the viewer with the same force as naturalistically rendered, material objects. An incidental effect, which may or may not have been part of Cézanne's original intention, but is important in twentieth-century developments from his art, is the "music" which the play of his line and color planes creates on his canvas. It can most easily be felt by turning a picture upside down, the *Forest with Rocks*, for instance (Plate 5), so that one's enjoyment of the abstract qualities of the composition need not be hindered by the pictorial reality.

Cézanne did away with traditional linear perspective as well as atmospheric perspective. His pictures are "flattened," the background drawn to the foreground rather than receding into the distance. This effort to interlock foreground and background into a unified pictorial construction is apparent in *The Gulf of Marseilles Seen from L'Estaque* (Plate 2).

Cézanne's portraits have little psychological interest. They are not character studies, but studies of form. Whether he painted a mountain, an apple, or a face, his interest was in form as revealed by color. Great patience was required of the subjects of his portraits, as they had to endure as many as a hundred sittings. Even then he seldom expressed satisfaction with the result. Regarding his *Portrait of Ambroise Vollard* (Plate 11) he remarked, after approximately a hundred sittings, that the triangle of shirt above the waistcoat was "not bad." His favorite subject, perhaps because it posed so satisfactorily, was the mountain of Sainte-Victoire, which he painted many times (Plate 8).

Still life was not, for Cézanne, a minor art form, but was treated with all the monumentality of his landscapes and figure compositions. In *Still Life with Plaster Cupid* (Plate 13) the cupid is clearly analyzed as a cluster of spheres, relating to the spheres of the apples and pears on the table. In order to flatten the composition, the diagonals of the tabletop spread as they recede instead of drawing together, so that the far edge of the table is longer and more prominent than the near side. The base of the plaster figure and the plate are likewise tipped toward the viewer, to lessen the feeling of depth.

When, after an isolation of twenty years, Cézanne finally had an exhibition in 1895 at Vollard's gallery, his works were a revelation to his fellow artists. Pissarro wrote: "My enthusiasm was as nothing compared to Renoir's. Even Degas was seduced by the charm of this refined savage. Monet, too — all of us." Renoir called the paintings "so crude and so admirable."

One of Cézanne's last paintings was *The Large Bathers* (Plate 12), on which he worked from 1898 until 1905, the year before his death. Here he is constructing a great architectural design. Figures, trees, and distant landscape are used, not for any interest in themselves, but only as parts of the design. They are distorted and interlocked to that end.

Many of Cézanne's sayings were as paradoxical as his art and his own character. Referring to his distortions he said: "One must master one's model," and, referring to his alteration of perspective and rearrangement of natural forms, "a powerful organizing mind is the best aid to sensation." But at another time and in another mood he would say: "One can never be too submissive to nature," and "if I think, everything is lost." On one point, however, he was unequivocal, and that was the difficulty of the aim he had set himself. A month before his death at sixty-seven, after a lifetime of unremitting effort, he wrote his son: "As a painter I am becoming more lucid in the presence of nature. But with me the realization of my sensations is always very hard. I cannot reach the intensity that I feel."

Gauguin

The reaction against realism and Impressionism, begun by Seurat and Cézanne, was carried on in a very different way by Gauguin. He had one artistic belief in

CÉZANNE *Still Life—Apples and Pears* (45 x 59 cm) New York, Metropolitan Museum of Art

GAUGUIN *Ia Orana Maria* (113.7 x 87.6 cm) New York, Metropolitan Museum of Art

8

common with Cézanne, that the two-dimensional quality of a canvas should be respected, that painting should not be treated as if it were sculpture. "A painting is a flat surface covered with colors arranged in a certain order." But in every other way the two men were at opposite poles.

The Symbolist literary movement was in vogue at the time. It preached a rebellion against naturalism and materialism. It was interested in the mysterious, the dreamlike, the irrational, rather than the natural, in suggestion and evocation rather than direct statement. There was an opening on the artistic scene for a Symbolist painter at precisely the moment when Gauguin appeared to fill it.

Gauguin showed no interest whatever in art until, as a successful stockbroker of twenty-five, he became a "Sunday painter" in the company of Émile Schuffenecker, a friend from his brokerage office. He was introduced to Pissarro, who became his friend and first teacher and through whom he met other Impressionist artists. Ten years later his interest had deepened to the point where he gave up his salaried position to devote himself entirely to painting.

His first works show the influence of Pissarro and his Impressionist friends (Plate 32), but this influence was soon superseded by that of the Symbolists. By symbolism is not meant anything as obvious as the skull to indicate death, the scythe for time, or the lily for purity. It was a symbolism of mood, of feeling, an effort to "clothe the idea in sensible form." Representation of reality ceased to be an end in itself and became a means to an end. Forms from real life are used to suggest and evoke, not to portray.

Gauguin's own style is first apparent in the paintings made in Brittany, where he had gone in the company of Émile Bernard. It is a style (called *cloisonnisme* after the *cloisonné* enamel technique) characterized by bright, flat color patterns and strong outlines used emotionally or decoratively rather than imitatively. It is intentionally primitive—Bernard and Gauguin set out to "paint like children"—and since Gauguin had no formal training other than what he had received from Pissarro, he had no sophisticated and artificial technique to unlearn.

A brief and disastrous stay with van Gogh at Arles produced a number of paintings, including *Old Women of Arles* (Plate 34), which illustrates this use of flat patterns of brilliant color within firm outlines. A strong influence from Japanese prints is apparent in the composition, particularly in the graceful, flowing diagonals and delicately leaved branches. "The eye seeks to refresh itself through your works," he said to his group of artist friends. "Give it food for enjoyment." Somewhat the same thought was expressed by van Gogh, but with the greater emotional depth that his painting has in comparison with Gauguin's: "I want to say something comforting in painting, as music is comforting."

Gauguin's search for the simple and primitive life eventually took him to Tahiti and the Marquesas Islands. There he confidently expected to live "on ecstasy, quiet and art, in amorous harmony with the mysterious beings around me." And so he did, if one accepts his paintings as truthful testimony of his South Sea idyll. The figures he portrays are indeed what he had expected Tahitian women to be: "Living statues from man's primeval age...clad only in sunbeams...walking always amid flowers." But what he created on canvas was his own dream world, not the world of bigoted French colonialism, of officialdom and missionaries and honky-tonk, of poverty and disease and pain and despair, which was what he really found in Tahiti.

Gauguin stretched truth in his writing, too, in order to support the dream world he had created in paint, and to stir up interest in it among collectors and the public. He even invented a picturesque, supposedly Polynesian theology to give his work authenticity. The idols that appear in some of his paintings have no basis in actuality, but are purely the products of his imagination—which does not matter, of course, as they completely fulfill their purpose.

His style changed very little, but the spirit of his art grew deeper, his color more resonant, his design simpler. A mood of mystery and of melancholy pervades his paintings. "It is extraordinary," the poet Mallarmé said of him, "that so much mystery can be combined with so much brilliance."

Gauguin was given to cryptic explanations of his work, which he frequently modified later on. Of *Nevermore* (Plate 40) he wrote: "Not 'The Raven' of Edgar Poe, but the bird of the Devil waiting his time....I have tried to suggest a certain bygone, barbaric splendor in a simple nude." But then he would say, with candid disparagement, "It is, after all, only a study of a nude from Oceania."

It is difficult to find much that is admirable in Gauguin as a man. His egotism was swollen to such a point that it filled his life: There was room for nothing else. "My family can stew in their own juice," he said. So, indeed, could everybody else. Nothing mattered except himself and his art. "I am a strong man and I can shape fate to my taste." But when it became quite evident that he could not control his fate, he faced that fact with a kind of flamboyant, exhibitionist courage that compels one's respect. At the peak of his Tahitian agony he wrote to a friend: "My resolution to end things is changed in the sense that nature is doing the job for me, though more slowly. I choke and vomit blood every day. My carcass is still resisting, but it is bound to break up—which is better than suicide, to which I should have been driven." He did, however, attempt suicide after all, but the dose of arsenic that he took was too strong; he vomited it up and crept back to his hut to live a little longer.

Degas, explaining to his friends the kind of man Gauguin was, alluded to the fable of La Fontaine, which compares the well-fed house dog and the lean and hungry wolf who refuses to accept comfort at the cost of a collar about his neck. "You see," Degas said, "Gauguin is the wolf."

Gauguin's contribution to art, aside from the paintings themselves, was, as one artist said in recognition of his debt, "to free us from all the restraints which the idea of copying nature had imposed upon us." Of this debt Gauguin said, with a modesty regarding his own work, which comes as a surprise, "I have attempted to establish the right to dare everything. The public owes me nothing, since my pictorial work is only relatively good, but the painters who now avail themselves of this freedom do owe me something."

Vincent van Gogh

How much Vincent van Gogh owed to Gauguin may be a matter of dispute. Certainly he was influenced by him in his use of flat color patterns and defined outlines. But the larger debt of which Gauguin speaks, "the right to dare everything," does not apply to van Gogh. Given his passionate character, his excessive sensitivity, the torment of his unrequited love for humanity, he would have found the freedom to express himself with or without Gauguin's example. For such a nature the emotional rather than representational use of color would have been instinctive.

In fact the word "Expressionism" was coined to describe van Gogh's work. He was the primitive of Expressionism. "I want to express," he said. "If people don't understand, I don't care." But the secret of his greatness was that he did care. He cared passionately.

Van Gogh's life was one long effort to give, to serve. "How can I be of some use in the world? Cannot I serve some purpose and be of some good?" He tried first as a lay preacher among the miners of the Borinage in Belgium. There he gave of himself so unstintingly, nursing, teaching, comforting, sharing what little he had — his food, his clothing, his blankets — that his embarrassed superiors recalled him.

The only requited love in his life, which was so full of outgoing love, was that for his brother, Theo. Theo believed in Vincent and supported him, as far as he was able, in all of his endeavors, and his letters to Theo form a diary of his life and a document of his art.

At this time, after his failure as a preacher, he turned to drawing. "I will take up my pencil," he wrote to Theo, "which I have forsaken in my great discouragement. I will go on with my drawing, and now everything seems transformed to me."

Van Gogh's early drawings and paintings were of the miners and peasants. He always identified with the humble and the unfortunate. *The Potato Eaters* was his first major effort. It is a dark and powerful painting whose every brush stroke is expressive of his great compassion. He tried, as he explained to Theo, to show that the knotted hands dipping into the bowl of potatoes have dug the earth, and to make the room smell of bacon fat and potato steam.

For a time he lived with Theo in Paris. Through his brother, who managed a branch of the Goupil art gallery, he met a number of Impressionist artists, including Pissarro, who is reported to have said of him, some years later: "I felt immediately that he would either go mad or surpass us all, but I didn't know that he would do both." Van Gogh adopted Impressionist colors and for a time experimented with Pointillist technique. His distinct, short brushstrokes made his canvases look like "fields of stubble."

He made the acquaintance of Père Tanguy, the gentle little seller of art supplies, in whose shop artists could always find a sympathetic viewer and sometimes a wall on which to display their work, and where indigent artists could exchange unsalable paintings for a supply of paint and canvas. Tanguy recognized greatness in van Gogh as he had in Cézanne, and they became good friends. One of the results of their friendship is the delightful *Portrait of Père Tanguy*, which plainly shows van Gogh's affection for the kindly, generous, and perceptive little man.

Two years in Paris completely transformed van Gogh's art. In 1888, longing for a simpler life and feeling that his continued presence might be a hindrance to his brother's career, he left for Arles in the south of France. Here, in what he called "the kingdom of light," he painted with violent passion and energy for the remaining two years of his life. His brushstroke was so broad and strong that even the surface of his canvas seems to vibrate with energy. He wrote Theo that he was not trying to reproduce exactly what he had before his eyes, but was using color more arbitrarily so as to express himself with more force. For the same purpose he was also distorting reality by exaggerating what he felt to be essential while leaving the surface detail vague. An example of such emotional use of color and distortion is his *Night Café* (Plate 51), in the blazing yellow and orange of the interior and the equally intense blue of the night sky with its enormous stars.

He rented a little house, his "yellow house," and prepared to welcome Gauguin, whom he had invited, through Theo's generosity, to visit him. Several years earlier, with love and despair and utter vulnerability, he had written Theo: "There may be a great fire in our soul and no one ever comes to warm himself at it, and the passersby see only a little bit of smoke coming through the chimney and go on their way….With how much patience, yet with how much impatience, must one wait for the hour when somebody will come and sit down near it—to stay there, maybe…." Now someone was coming, the first, he hoped, of many who would make the yellow house the "House of Friends."

The visit was a disaster. Gauguin's egotism and overbearing ways, and van Gogh's emotional sensitivity and lack of balance made some sort of explosion inevitable. Van Gogh succumbed to the first of the recurrent attacks of madness that caused his confinement for a year in the hospital at Saint-Rémy.

There he continued to paint. His canvases, particularly those of cypresses, which he painted many times, as if he felt a peculiar affinity for them, (Plate 50), show in their writhing, twisting forms against turbulent skies the torment of his repeated seizures.

He moved to a private sanatorium at Auvers-sur-Oise, not far from Paris, and there in 1890, at the age of thirty-seven, he took his own life. Theo outlived him by only six months, and the two brothers are buried side by side in the cemetery at Auvers.

Van Gogh's career as a mature artist lasted only five years. But in spite of its brevity, the art that it produced has been a major influence on painting of the twentieth century. Critics dispute his stature as an artist, although his influence is indisputable. Those who prefer a more balanced and ordered art consider him only second-rate. Others, and they are the majority, consider that his mental instability may have been the key to the emotional expressiveness that, for them, constitutes his genius. In any case his art is greatly loved. Many have come to warm themselves at his fire.

After Theo's death the proprietor of the Goupil gallery in which he had worked installed a new manager. "Our late manager," he said, "a madman of sorts, like his brother the painter…accumulated appalling things by modern painters. Do the best you can with these horrors." The "horrors" were works by Degas, van Gogh, Gauguin, and Lautrec, and the new manager, Maurice Joyant, who had been a schoolmate of Lautrec, promptly asked him to submit more pictures.

Toulouse-Lautrec
Henri-Marie-Raymond de Toulouse-Lautrec was the son of a provincial count.

In his early teens two accidents stunted the growth of his legs, so that as he matured his torso and head developed normally, but his legs did not. He had enjoyed drawing since childhood, and after his accident he turned to it more and more. His earliest paintings, done when he was only sixteen years old, are mostly of sporting subjects. One of these paintings shows his father, Count Alphonse, driving a diligence at Nice, where the family often went for the winter (Plate 52). It is a remarkable achievement for such a young artist, and already shows several of the characteristics that distinguish his mature art. One of these is his tremendous feeling for action, and another is his ability to sense and to portray the point in that action that is most typical of it. The figure of his father, tense, reckless, his enthusiasm in droll contrast with his dignity, is caught at just such a moment. Another Lautrec characteristic is the introduction into the painting of figures not directly involved in the action, whose very inactivity heightens its effect, as the servant with folded arms, sitting behind Count Alphonse, heightens by his almost uninterested inactivity the old aristocrat's eagerness.

At the age of eighteen Lautrec obtained his family's permission to become a professional artist, and his mother arranged a studio for him in her Paris apartment. He studied briefly at several art schools, in one of which he met van Gogh. While their dramatically different characters made impossible any deep friendship between them, Lautrec must have admired and respected van Gogh, because a few years later, at an exhibition in Belgium, he challenged a Belgian artist to a duel for speaking disparagingly of van Gogh's work.

As a child Lautrec had received a book on falconry from his father with an inscription on the flyleaf: "Remember, my son, that life in the open air and the light of day is the only healthy one." Ironically, Lautrec lived so exclusively at night that daylight would have hurt his eyes. His grotesquely dwarfish appearance and his ugly face shut him off from conventional society and impelled him toward the "night people" of Paris, and particularly of Montmartre—the actors and actresses, circus performers, dancers, nightclub entertainers, pimps and prostitutes. Those were the subjects and that was the life that he painted. For him an interest in the unnatural effects of artificial light replaced the Impressionist interest in effects of sunlight and atmosphere. He was the chronicler of the frenzied gaiety of Parisian night life as the Impressionists had been of the pastimes of the Parisian bourgeoisie in the healthy light of day. And he lived the life he depicted—he was its rather pathetic hero.

A cousin of Lautrec's and his constant companion in his night adventures was Dr. Gabriel Tapié de Céleyran. A more fantastic pair would be difficult to imagine. Both were rather dandified in dress, de Céleyran tall and thin, wearing formal clothes and a top hat, which accentuated his height, Lautrec in a morning coat, pale trousers, and a bowler hat, which set off his compact squatness. Nightly they toured the theaters, music halls, cafés, and circuses. According to his friends' reports, Lautrec was an extrovert, gay, witty, and energetic, in spite of his handicap an ideal companion for a night's carouse. But for him it was a lifetime's carouse. He lived as though he sensed that his life would not be long.

His portrait of his cousin and companion (Plate 54) shows Lautrec's superb gift for characterization. Not the face alone, but the pose of the entire figure is involved in this characterization. This he derives from Degas, whom he much admired. Both artists could express personality in a few typical gestures. Both, too, were influenced by Japanese prints in their use of a high horizon, diagonal movement, and off-center placement of important pictorial elements, as here and in the following three plates, 55, 56, and 57. Typical of Lautrec's own style, and quite apart from Degas, is his reduction of figures to expressive silhouettes while retaining a sense of their mass, as in the portrait of de Céleyran and the drawing of one of his favorite performers, Chocolat, dancing in the Bar d'Achille (Plate 57). He simplified almost to the point of caricature, but not quite.

In subject matter Lautrec was far more daring than Degas. Accepting no taboos, he lived in brothels and painted portraits of prostitutes, not for any effect of sensationalism, but simply because he considered human degradation as fit a subject for art as any other. In *The Salon in the Rue des Moulins* (Plate 56) the subject is treated in a completely objective and inoffensive way, clinically, without compassion but also without viciousness. There is never any emotion in Lautrec's work. It is as if his physical abnormality had cut him off from normal human feeling as well as from conventional society. His work has animation, excitement, and action, but no emotion. In fact, his view is so detached that, without knowledge of the facts of his life, one would say he had been an observer only, rather than a participator in the life he portrays.

In 1893 Lautrec was given a show by his friend and classmate Joyant at the Goupil gallery. Degas, visiting it, commented, "So, Lautrec, it's plain that you and I agree!" His father was displeased, however, and begged him "for the honor of the family name" not to paint any more Montmartre subjects.

Eventually the dissipation of Lautrec's life, which for years had seemed to sharpen his faculties rather than to dim them, began to affect his mind. After a period in a sanatorium, being treated for alcoholism, he was released, and returned to Paris. He celebrated his return characteristically, with a party. The invitations asked his friends to come to his studio and share a glass of milk with him, and were decorated with a cartoon showing him milking a cow.

Lautrec's greatest art is to be found not in his painting, but in his lithographs. In this medium he is unsurpassed. He might have been a greater painter, perhaps, if he had been less talented. His great facility ran away with him. He is a commentator of great wit and style, but often his work has something of illustration in it that diminishes it. A new, broader, less illustrative style shows itself in one of the last paintings he made, *An Examination at the Faculty of Medicine* (Plate 60). But it is useless to speculate on what might have developed from it, as death ended his career in 1901. Like van Gogh, he was thirty-seven years old. His candle had burned at both ends, but with a bright, dispassionate light very different from Vincent's fire.

PLATES

Paul Cézanne

PLATE 1   PAUL CÉZANNE *The House of the Hanged Man, Auvers (La Maison du Pendu),* 1873 (55.5 x 66.5 cm) Paris, Louvre

PLATE 2 PAUL CÉZANNE *The Gulf of Marseilles Seen from L'Estaque*, 1883–85 (73 x 100 cm) New York, Metropolitan Museum of Art, Havemeyer Collection

PLATE 3 PAUL CÉZANNE *Zola's House at Medan*, c. 1880 (59 x 72 cm) Glasgow, Art Gallery and Museum, Burrell Collection

PLATE 4 PAUL CÉZANNE *The Park of Le Chateau Noir*, Paris, Louvre

PLATE 5 PAUL CÉZANNE *Forest with Rocks*, c. 1895 (48.5 x 59.5 cm) Zürich, Kunsthaus

23

PLATE 6 PAUL CÉZANNE *Woman with Coffeepot,* 1893–94 (130.5 x 96.5 cm) Paris, Louvre (Gift of M. and Mme J. V. Pellerin)

PLATE 7 PAUL CÉZANNE *Old Woman with Rosary* (85 x 65 cm) London, National Gallery

PLATE 8 PAUL CÉZANNE *Mont Sainte-Victoire*, 1904–1906 (73 x 92 cm) Philadelphia, Museum of Art, George W. Elkins Collection

PLATE 9 PAUL CÉZANNE *Le Cabanon de Jourdan*, 1906 (65 x 81 cm) Milan, private collection

PLATE 10   PAUL CÉZANNE *The Red Vest*, c. 1895 (79.5 x 64 cm) Zürich, E. Bührle Collection

PLATE 11   PAUL CÉZANNE *Portrait of Ambroise Vollard*, 1899 (100 x 81 cm) Paris, Musée du Petit Palais, Vollard Collection

29

PLATE 12 PAUL CÉZANNE *The Large Bathers*, 1898–1905 (208 x 251 cm) Philadelphia, Museum of Art. P. Wilstach Collection

PLATE 13 PAUL CÉZANNE *Still Life with Plaster Cupid*, c. 1895 (63 x 81 cm) Stockholm, Nationalmuseum

Seurat and Divisionism

PLATE 14   GEORGES SEURAT *Bathing at Asnières*, 1883–84 (201 x 301.5 cm) London, Tate Gallery

PLATE 15   GEORGES SEURAT *The Shore at Bas-Butin, Honfleur*, 1886 (66 x 82 cm) Tournai, Musée des Beaux-Arts

PLATE 16   GEORGES SEURAT *Study for "La Grande-Jatte,"* 1884–85 (70.5 x 104.2 cm) New York, Metropolitan Museum of Art (Bequest
of Samuel A. Lewisohn)

PLATE 17 GEORGES SEURAT *A Sunday Afternoon on the Island of La Grande-Jatte*, 1884–86 (205.7 x 305.8 cm) Chicago, Art Institute of Chicago, Helen Birch Bartlett Memorial Collection

PLATE 18   PAUL SIGNAC *The Seine at Asnières*, 1885 (73 x 100 cm) Paris, from the collection of Mme Ginette Signac

PLATE 19   ALBERT DUBOIS-PILLET *Village near Bonnières*, 1885 (33 x 55 cm) Geneva, Oscar Ghez Foundation of Modern Art

PLATE 20   PAUL SIGNAC *Two Milliners*, 1885 (100 x 81 cm) Zürich, E. Bührle Collection

PLATE 21   PAUL SIGNAC *The Côte-d'Azur.* 1889 (66 x 81 cm) The Hague, Gemeentemuseum, Haags Collection

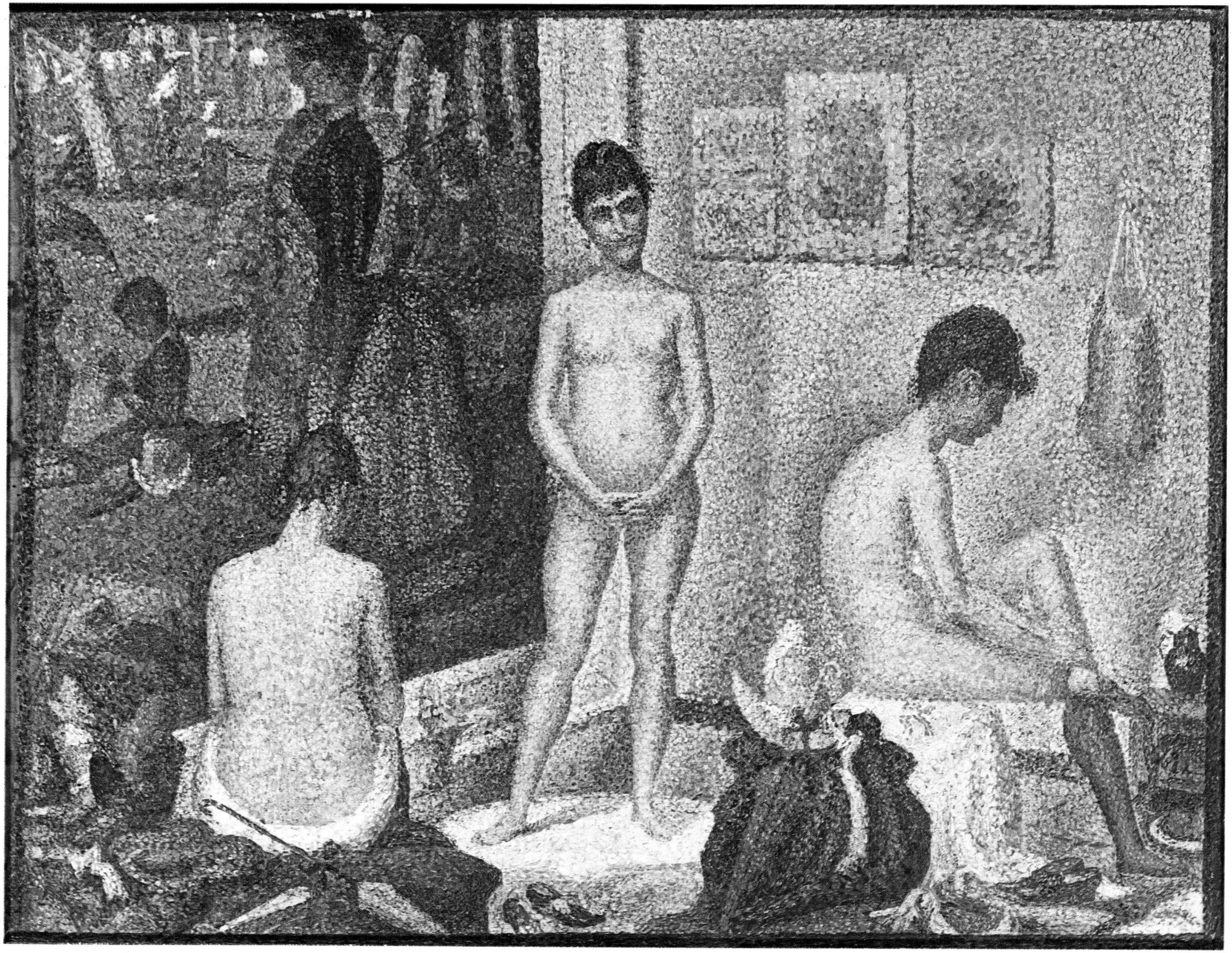

PLATE 22 GEORGES SEURAT *The Models* (small version) 1888 (39.4 x 48.9 cm) Philadelphia, Henry P. McIlhenny Collection

PLATE 23   GEORGES SEURAT *Sunday, Port-en-Bessin*, 1888 (66 x 82 cm) Otterlo, Rijksmuseum Kröller-Müller

PLATE 24   THÉO VAN RYSSELBERGHE *Portrait of Mme Rysselberghe*, 1892 (186 x 97 cm)
Otterlo, Rijksmuseum Kröller-Müller

PLATE 25   HENRI-EDMOND CROSS *Portrait of Mme Cross* (95 x 75 cm) Paris, Musée National d'Art Moderne

PLATE 26   Albert Dubois-Pillet *The Marne at Dawn* (32 x 46 cm) Paris, Musée National d'Art Moderne

PLATE 27   CHARLES ANGRAND *The Seine at Dawn*, 1889 (65 x 81 cm) Geneva, Oscar Ghez Foundation of Modern Art

45

PLATE 28   HENRI-EDMOND CROSS *The Golden Islands*, c. 1891–92 (60 x 55 cm) Paris, Musée National d'Art Moderne

PLATE 29   GEORGES SEURAT *Young Woman Powdering Herself*, 1889–90 (94.5 x 79.2 cm) London, Courtauld Institute

PLATE 30   Henry van de Velde *Twilight*, 1892 (45 x 60 cm) Otterlo, Rijksmuseum Kröller-Müller

PLATE 31   MAXIMILIEN LUCE *View of Montmartre*, 1887 (45.5 x 81 cm) Otterlo, Rijksmuseum Kröller-Müller

49

Gauguin and the Pont-Aven School

PLATE 32   PAUL GAUGUIN *The Seine near the Iéna Bridge,* 1875 (64 x 92 cm) Paris, Louvre

PLATE 33   PAUL GAUGUIN *Landscape at Le Pouldu, Brittany,* 1890 (73.3 x 92.3 cm) Upperville, Va., Mr. and Mrs. Paul
Mellon Collection

PLATE 34   PAUL GAUGUIN *Old Women of Arles,* 1888 (73 x 91.5 cm) Chicago, Art Institute of Chicago, Mr. and Mrs. Lewis
L. Coburn Memorial Collection

PLATE 35   LOUIS ROY *Washerwomen,* 1895 (17 x 23.5 cm) private collection

PLATE 36   EMILE BERNARD *Stoneware Vases and Apples,* 1887 (46 x 55 cm) Paris, Musée National d'Art Moderne

PLATE 37   JACOB MEYER DE HAAN *Still Life with Carrots*, 1889–90 (60 x 73 cm) Paris, Musée National d'Art Moderne

PLATE 38   CHARLES LAVAL *Landscape* (55 x 46 cm) Paris, Musée National d'Art Moderne

PLATE 39   EMILE BERNARD *The Flight into Egypt*, 1889 (50 x 64 cm) Milan, Galleria del Levante

PLATE 40 PAUL GAUGUIN *Nevermore*, 1897 (59.5 x 117 cm) London, Courtauld Institute

58

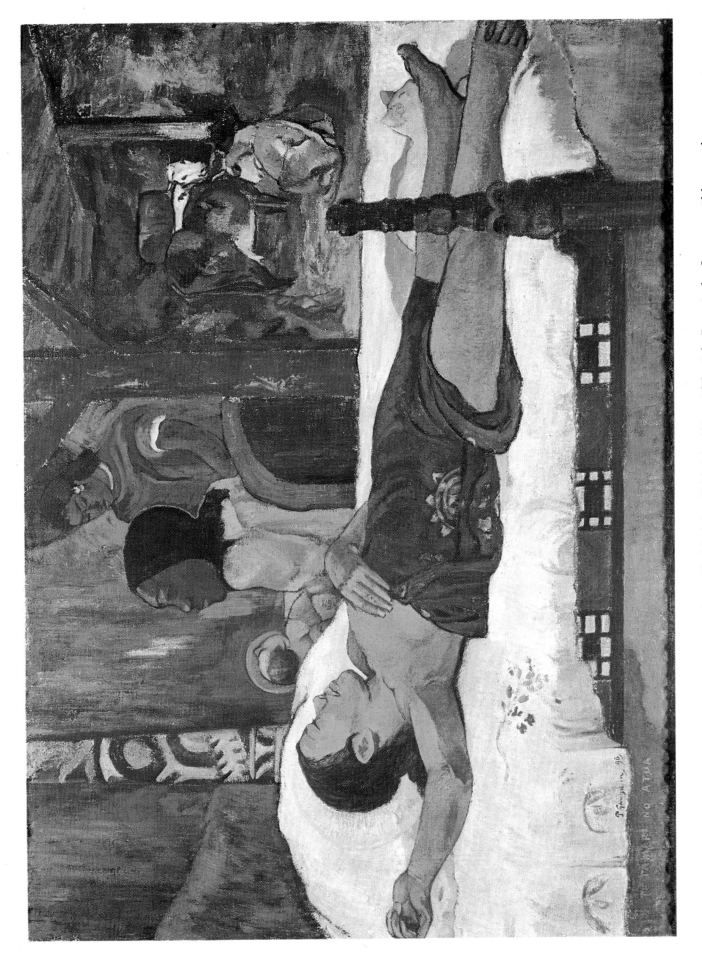

PLATE 41 PAUL GAUGUIN *Te Tamari No Atua: The Nativity,* 1896 (96 x 129 cm) Munich, Bayerische Staatsgemäldesammlungen

PLATE 42 PAUL GAUGUIN *Tahitian Women on the Beach*, 1891 (69 x 90 cm) Paris, Louvre

PLATE 43   PAUL GAUGUIN *Two Tahitian Women*, 1899 (94 x 73 cm) New York, Metropolitan Museum of Art (Gift of William Church Osborn)

Vincent van Gogh

PLATE 44   VINCENT VAN GOGH *The Bathing Float, Paris,* C. 1887 (19 x 27 cm) Upperville, Va., Mr. and Mrs. Paul Mellon
Collection

PLATE 45   Vincent van Gogh *The Drawbridge at Arles (Le Pont de L'Anglois)*, 1888 (49 x 64.5 cm) Cologne, Wallraf-Richartz-Museum

PLATE 46   VINCENT VAN GOGH *Boats at Les Saintes-Maries,* 1888 (66 x 81.5 cm) Amsterdam, Stedelijk Museum, Vincent van Gogh Foundation Collection

PLATE 47   VINCENT VAN GOGH *La Mousme*, 1888 (74 x 60 cm) Washington, D.C., National Gallery of Art, Chester Dale Collection

PLATE 48   Vincent van Gogh *The Artist's Bedroom at Arles*, 1889 (72 x 91 cm) Amsterdam, Stedelijk Museum, Vincent van Gogh Foundation Collection

PLATE 49 Vincent van Gogh *Still Life with Drawing Board and Onions*, 1889 (50 x 64 cm) Otterlo, Rijksmuseum Kröller-Müller

67

PLATE 50 VINCENT VAN GOGH *Cypresses*, 1889 (95.5 x 73.5 cm) New York, Metropolitan Museum of Art, Rogers Fund

PLATE 51   VINCENT VAN GOGH *Night Café,* 1888 (89 x 70 cm) New Haven, Conn., Yale University, S. C. Clark Collection

Henri de Toulouse-Lautrec

PLATE 52   HENRI DE TOULOUSE-LAUTREC *Count Alphonse de Toulouse-Lautrec Driving the Mail Coach at Nice*, 1881 (43 x 52 cm)
Paris, Musée du Petit Palais

PLATE 53   HENRI DE TOULOUSE-LAUTREC *The Laundress*, 1889 (93 x 75 cm) Paris, private collection

PLATE 54   HENRI DE TOULOUSE-LAUTREC *Dr. Gabriel Tapié de Céleyran at the
Comédie Française,* 1894 (110 x 56 cm) Albi, Musée Toulouse-Lautrec

PLATE 55   HENRI DE TOULOUSE-LAUTREC *Jane Avril Dancing*, c. 1892 (85 x 45 cm)
Paris, Louvre

PLATE 56   HENRI DE TOULOUSE-LAUTREC *Pastel Study for "The Salon in the Rue des Moulins,"* 1894 (111 x 132 cm) Albi, Musée
Toulouse-Lautrec

PLATE 57   HENRI DE TOULOUSE-LAUTREC *Chocolat Dancing in the Bar d'Achille*, 1896 (77 x 61 cm) Albi, Musée Toulouse-Lautrec

PLATE 58   HENRI DE TOULOUSE-LAUTREC *Woman at Her Toilette: Mme Poupoule*, 1898 (60 x 40 cm) Albi, Musée Toulouse-Lautrec

PLATE 59   HENRI DE TOULOUSE-LAUTREC *The Bed,* c. 1892–95 (53 x 70 cm) Paris, Louvre

PLATE 60   HENRI DE TOULOUSE-LAUTREC *An Examination at tne Faculty of Medicine,* 1901 (63 x 79 cm) Albi, Musée Toulouse-Lautrec

THE ARTISTS

CHARLES ANGRAND

Born at Criquetot-sur-Ouville, April 29, 1854. After completing his studies he worked as a private instructor at Rouen and then at Paris.

He was one of the group of painters who gathered around Seurat and who began the Divisionist or Neo-Impressionist movement. Like Signac and Cross, he was active in arranging the first exhibitions of the Independent Artists.

He died at seventy-one in Rouen, April 1, 1926.

EMILE BERNARD

Born at Lille in 1868. At sixteen he enrolled at the studio of Cormon in Paris, where he met Louis Anquetin, Toulouse-Lautrec, and van Gogh. In 1886 he went to Pont-Aven in Brittany, where he made the acquaintance of Gauguin. Two years later he was one of the principal figures in the group of painters who surrounded Gauguin at Pont-Aven. In 1889 Bernard contributed more than twenty paintings to the show at Volpini's *Café des Arts* along with Gauguin, Anquetin, Laval, and others.

In 1891 he quarreled with Gauguin and during the years from 1893 to 1904 he lived principally in Cairo, spending short periods in Venice and Spain. He studied the artists of the Italian Renais-

BERNARD *Self-Portrait*, 1888 (46 x 55 cm) Amsterdam, Stedelijk Museum, Vincent van Gogh Foundation Collection

sance, whom he deeply admired, and in his effort to imitate them he lost the strength and originality of his own style, lapsing into academicism.

He was a critic of some note; he collaborated on the reviews *Mercure de France* and *L'Occident*, and founded one himself, *La Rénovation Esthétique* He died at Paris in 1941.

CÉZANNE *Self-Portrait*, 1879–82 (65 x 51 cm) Bern Kunstmuseum

PAUL CÉZANNE

Born January 19, 1839, at Aix-en-Provence, of a well-to-do family. In 1852 at Bourbon College he met Émile Zola; they were friends for more than thirty years. He also attended art school.

Cézanne wanted to go to Paris to study painting, but his father's opposition prevented him from carrying out his wish until 1861. His first stay in Paris was not, however, a happy one. Disillusioned and embittered, he returned after a few months to Aix, where he worked in his father's bank. But at the end of 1862 he was back in Paris, where he frequented the Swiss Academy and struck up friendships with many of the future Impressionists: Pissarro, Monet, Sisley, Renoir, and others. Discouraged again, he returned to Aix in 1864. From then until 1870 he lived alternately in Paris and Aix. At the outbreak of the Franco-Prussian War in 1870 he retired to L'Estaque, near Marseilles, to paint. In 1872–73 he joined Pissarro at Auvers-sur-Oise, where he painted *The House of the Hanged Man, Auvers*, which he exhibited the following year, with other canvases, at the first Impressionist Show. His works were given a very poor reception by the public both then and at the third Impressionist Show in 1877, in which

Cézanne *Card Player*, 1890–92 (36.3 x 48.5 cm) Chicago, Chauncey McCormick Collection

Cézanne *Seated Peasant*, 1900– 1904 (45 x 30 cm) Zürich, Kunsthaus

Fair, and in 1890 at Brussels, at a show organized by the Belgian group *Les XX* — "The Twenty." (This group, organized in 1884, made it their policy to invite foreign avant-garde artists to send paintings to their exhibitions.) Cézanne's first one-man show, arranged in 1895 by a dealer, Ambroise Vollard, although it again failed to make his painting understood by the public, increased its appreciation by artists. By the beginning of this century his fame was international; he showed at Brussels with the Independents and with great success at the Autumn Show.

On October 15, 1906, caught in a rainstorm as he was painting, he came down with a fever and died on October 22, at the age of sixty-seven.

HENRI-EDMOND CROSS

Born at Douai in 1856, as Henri-Edmond Delacroix, he later changed his name, perhaps to

Luce *Portrait of Henri-Edmond Cross*, c. 1890, New York, private collection

avoid confusion with Eugène Delacroix. He studied at the Academy of Fine Arts at Lille and later enrolled at the studio of Bonvin in Paris. He became acquainted with Impressionism, but later adopted the Divisionist technique of Seurat and Signac. He participated in the exhibitions of the Independents. His rich colors, decorative taste, and free interpretation of representational sub-

he exhibited seventeen paintings. The following year he withdrew from the Impressionist group.

Beside Aix and Paris he worked at L'Estaque, Pontoise, Fontainebleau, and Giverny. In 1886 occurred his break with Zola, who in his novel *L'Oeuvre* used Cézanne as the model for one of his characters, an unsuccessful painter.

A few years earlier, in 1882, one of Cézanne's works had been accepted by the annual, "official" Paris Salon; in 1889, thanks to the collector Victor Chocquet, Cézanne exhibited at the Paris World

MEYER DE HAAN *Self-Portrait in a Breton Costume*
(72 x 55 cm) Denis Collection

jects lead him to be considered one of the precursors of Fauvism. He died at Saint-Clair, in the south of France, in 1910.

JACOB MEYER DE HAAN

Born in 1852 at Amsterdam. Spent his youth in London, where he made the acquaintance of Pissarro. Through him he met Gauguin, whom he joined at Pont-Aven in 1888 and with whom he quickly formed a friendship. In 1889 he was with Gauguin at Le Pouldu, in Brittany, where there also gathered Paul Sérusier, Laval, and Charles Filliger. Generous with financial help to his teacher-friend, he returned to Le Pouldu in 1890; his house was Gauguin's studio. The following year he met the painter Jan Verkade and introduced him to Gauguin and the Symbolists.

When Gauguin decided to leave for the tropics he repeatedly invited de Haan to go with him, but the latter decided against it. Four years later, in 1895, Meyer de Haan died at Amsterdam, in his early forties.

ALBERT DUBOIS-PILLET

Born at Paris, October 28, 1845. He embarked on a military career and became an officer of the Republican Guard. It was he who, after having exhibited with the Group of Independent Artists in 1884, had the idea of forming a "Society of Independent Artists," which was founded in June of that year by Seurat, Signac, and Odilon Redon. In 1888 he was invited to exhibit with "The Twenty" (*Les XX*) at Brussels, along with Signac and Cross. At that time several Belgian painters, who had been impressed by the works of Seurat that had been shown there the year before, joined the Divisionists.

Dubois-Pillet was represented at all the shows of the Independents from the first to the one in 1890, the year of his early death at Le Puy. At the Independent Show of 1891 he was given a retrospective exhibit at which over sixty canvases were displayed.

PAUL GAUGUIN

Born in Paris, June 7, 1848. As a child he spent four years in Peru with his family. Having returned to Orléans in France, he completed regular studies and then, in 1865, went to sea. In 1871 he joined the brokerage office of Bertin, and in 1873 married a Danish girl, Mette-Sophie Gad. On his free days he painted in the company of his colleague Émile Schuffenecker. In 1876 one of his paintings was accepted by the Salon, and from 1880 on he took part in all the Impressionist shows. At this time he had to choose between his responsibilities at work and home, and his wish to paint full-time. At the beginning of 1883, without even telling his wife, he left his work, consumed by the sole, almost insane desire to paint. To follow his vocation he had to contend with everything: with his family, whom he abandoned in Copenhagen after an unfortunate attempt there to reconcile business and

GAUGUIN *Van Gogh Painting Sunflowers*, 1888, Amsterdam, Stedelijk Museum, Vincent van Gogh Foundation Collection

art, and with poverty, illness, and public indifference or scorn.

In June of 1885 he began his frequent journeys between Paris and Brittany. In Brittany he met Charles Laval, with whom he made his first escape from civilization. They left in April 1887 for Panama, then Martinique, but in November, ill and discouraged, they were back in Paris without a cent. Generously, Schuffenecker came to Gauguin's aid and took him into his home. Gauguin met Vincent van Gogh again, with his brother, Theo, who was enthusiastic about his work, and in the Goupil gallery, which Theo managed, he held a show in 1888, but without commercial success. Meanwhile, Gauguin was again settled at Pont-Aven in Brittany, painting, carving, making ceramics, surrounded by a group of artists including young Bernard, Laval, de Haan, and Sérusier.

After his visit with van Gogh at Arles, with its dramatic ending, he went to Paris, then left again for Brittany. The show at the Café Volpini in 1889 was another fiasco, but his researches aroused interest among painters and critics. At the end of 1890 he was in Paris and frequented the Symbolist meetings at the Café Voltaire, where he met Mallarmé, Aurier, Morice, Redon, Carrière, Mirbeau, and the Nabis group.

In 1891 he made up his mind to leave France for the tropics. His first stay at Tahiti was neither long nor happy, but still he was drawn by the climate, natural life, and freedom. In Paris, where he returned to live from August of 1893 to February of 1895, he met with nothing but disappointments: His show at the Durand-Ruel Gallery failed, his

GAUGUIN *L'Arlésienne*,1888 (47.5 x 55 cm)
Bradford, Pa., T. Edward Hanley Collection

GAUGUIN *Soyez Amoureuses Vous Serez Heureuses*, Chicago, Art Institute of Chicago

auction sale was a disaster, his visit to his wife at Copenhagen led nowhere, an inheritance from his uncle was soon spent, and after a drunken fight with some sailors, during which he was injured, Anna, his Javanese mistress, plundered his studio and ran off.

He left again for Tahiti at the beginning of 1895, never to return to France. Alone and in great suffering, he attempted suicide in 1898. Because of trouble with the island authorities, he left Tahiti in 1901 for Dominica in the Marquesas Islands. There, gravely ill, he thought for a moment of returning to France. Again he got into trouble with the authorities and was sentenced, in March of 1903, to a fine and three months' imprisonment. Overwhelmed by all these troubles, consumed by disease, consoled only by the protestant pastor Vernier, his neighbor, he died on May 8, 1903.

GAUGUIN
Noa-Noa, Paris,
Louvre

CHARLES LAVAL

Born in 1862, his brief life ended in 1894 at Cairo. In 1886, at the Pension Gloanec at Pont-Aven, where he was living and painting, he met Paul Gauguin. A firm friendship was quickly established between the two artists; in April of the following year, when Gauguin decided to leave for Panama to live a primitive life in contact with nature, Laval went with him. When Laval came down with yellow fever at Panama the two left for Martinique, where Gauguin, in his turn, fell ill. In November, sick and without a penny, they returned to Paris.

In 1888 Laval, Bernard, and other young painters worked with Gauguin at Pont-Aven, forming the group that came to be called the School of Pont-Aven. A year later, with Gauguin and others, including Bernard, Louis Roy, and Schuffenecker, he exhibited in the show that the latter organized at the Café Volpini in Paris.

MAXIMILIEN LUCE

Born in Paris in 1858. Attended the Academy of Fine Arts, student of Carolus Duran. In 1887 he joined the Divisionists and took part in the show of the Independents; he exhibited with them regularly during the years following. A good friend of Seurat, he had difficulty subjugating his romantic temperament to the rigorous Divisionist technique.

He frequented the offices of the *Revue Indépendante* (on whose premises his first one-man show was held) where other Divisionist painters

LUCE *Portrait of Georges Seurat*, 1890 (24.5 x 21 cm) Paris, from the collection of Frédéric Luce

and friends of the critic Félix Fénéon congregated. With Fénéon he was implicated in a famous trial against thirty anarchists. He worked as an artist for several periodicals. Died in Paris, 1941.

GEORGES SEURAT

Born in Paris in December of 1859. In 1878 he enrolled at the Academy of Fine Arts. He came under the influence of Ingres, Eugène Delacroix, and Puvis de Chavannes, and was deeply im-

SEURAT *Standing Model (study for "The Models")*, 1886–87, Paris, Louvre

LAVAL *Self-Portrait*, 1888, Amsterdam, Stedelijk Museum, Vincent van Gogh Foundation Collection

pressed by the fourth Impressionist exhibition. As a young man he was interested in the scientific treatises of Chevreul and other scientists, and tried to apply these theories to painting. From 1881 to 1883 he dedicated himself to working solely in black and white.

His first large painting, *Bathing at Asnières*, was rejected by the 1884 Salon, but he exhibited it at the show of the Group of Independent Artists the same year. At the meetings for the formation of the Society of Independent Artists, of which he was one of the founders, he met Paul Signac. In collaboration with Signac, Seurat perfected the system of his new technique. Its fruit is *A Sunday Afternoon on the Island of La Grande-Jatte*, on which he worked for two years.

In 1886 Camille Pissarro, who for some time, followed by his son Lucien, had adhered to Seurat's ideas, managed with some difficulty to get him and Signac admitted to the eighth Impressionist

SEURAT *The Coachman*, c. 1882, Paris, from the collection of Mme H. Bérès

show. Seurat exhibited, with other works, his *Grande-Jatte*, which was met by derision from both public and critics. Few appreciated it; among those who did were van Gogh, the Belgian symbolist poet Verhaeren, and above all the critic Félix Fénéon, who became the champion of the movement, which he named Neo-Impressionism. Seurat exhibited the *Grande-Jatte* again at the Independent show that year, and the following year in Brussels with *Les XX*, with whom he showed again in 1889 and 1891. Meanwhile a group of artists was forming around Seurat, adhering to the principles of Divisionism, but developing their own personal styles: Beside Signac and the two Pissarros there were Dubois-Pillet, Angrand, Cross, Luce, Léo Gausson, Hippolyte Petitjean, and the Belgians Willy Finch, van Rysselberghe, and Georges Lemmen. Around 1890 the group showed its first signs of disintegration, and Pissarro and others abandoned the movement. From 1886 Seurat was impressed by the theories

SEURAT *Singer at the Café-Concert*, 1887, Amsterdam, Stedelijk Museum

on the aesthetic and emotional effect of line and color, logically used, of Charles Henry, whose influence is easily recognizable in *The Parade* (1887–88), *Le Chahut* (1889–90), and *The Circus* (1890–91). On March 29, 1891, Seurat died in Paris.

PAUL SIGNAC

Born in Paris, November 11, 1863, of a bourgeois family. He quickly showed a keen interest in the

SEURAT *The Artist's Father (Le Dineur)*, c. 1884, Paris, private collection

most advanced artistic and political trends. In 1883 he enrolled at Bin's studio, but meanwhile he assiduously studied the works of the Impressionists. The following year he exhibited at the show of the Group of Independent Artists and founded, with Seurat and Redon, the Society of Independent Artists. His meeting with Georges Seurat was decisive for his future stylistic development. Seurat's color researches, in combination with Signac's own, resulted in the development of the Divisionist technique. In 1886, thanks to the intercession of Pissarro, he and Seurat were accepted at the eighth Impressionist exhibition. In the meantime he became associated with the literary Symbolists and the critic Fénéon, champion of the Divisionist movement, and shared Seurat's interest in the theories of Charles Henry.

Signac was a critic too, collaborating on several periodicals, and wrote *From Eugène Delacroix to Neo-Impressionism* (1899), the culmination of his defense of the Neo-Impressionist movement, whose leader he became after Seurat's death.

The period from 1887 to 1890 was the most productive for Signac: He exhibited at the Independents' annual shows and at those of *Les XX* in 1888, 1890, and 1891. After 1890 he made many trips abroad, and as he was a keen sailor he depicted ports in both watercolors and oils.

In 1908 he was elected president of the Society of Independent Artists, and gave himself to his duties with great zeal for twenty-six years. He died in Paris, August 15, 1935.

SIGNAC *Application of a Chromatic Circle,* Boston, Museum of Fine Arts (Gift of Peter A. Wick)

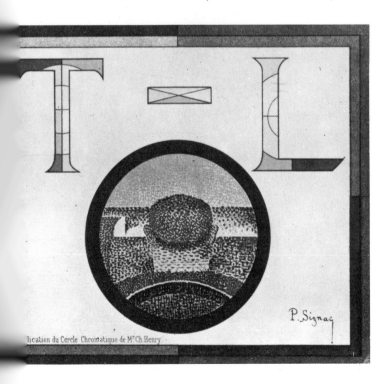

HENRI DE TOULOUSE-LAUTREC

Born at Albi, November 24, 1864, of aristocratic family. In 1872 he moved with his family to Paris. Sketches of horses and caricatures of professors and friends are proof, even at that time, of an outstanding talent with brush and pencil. But per-

SIGNAC *Woman at the Window (study for "Parisian Sunday"),* Paris, from the collection of Mme Ginette Signac

haps such a talent would never have exceeded an elegant dilettantism if two accidents in close succession (1878 and 1879) had not unexpectedly upset young Henri's life. As a result of two serious falls his legs were broken and ceased to develop. In drawing, however, he found the means to combat the boredom of the long hours of immobility. Encouraged by René Princeteau, a deaf-mute painter who was a friend of his father's, he asked to be permitted to devote himself to painting.

In 1882 he enrolled at the studio of Léon Bonnat, one of the painters of "official" taste currently popular in Paris, and stayed there until the following spring. He spent the summer at Albi, painting portraits that are evidence of his notable technical progress. Back in Paris he attended Cormon's studio, where he stayed until 1886 and struck up friendships with many of his classmates, among them Bernard and van Gogh.

In 1884 he rented a studio in Montmartre, where he stayed until 1897. In the bohemian quarter of Montmartre he discovered his world. The frenetic, carefree, and bitter life there offered continual inpetus to his curiosity and to his restless brush. In 1893 he exhibited at the Goupil Gallery the works inspired by his Montmartre surroundings. The show had a moderate success and received the approval of the great Degas. The theater also attracted Lautrec, and for theatrical performances he designed programs and posters, and made paintings and lithographs of famous actors and actresses. His friend Tristan Bernard introduced him to the world of sport, where he found new interests and enthusiasms.

In 1895 he went to London and there met Whistler and Oscar Wilde. The following year he traveled in Holland, Belgium, Spain, and Portugal, broadening his knowledge of art. He joined the group of *La Revue Blanche* and made many friends there, in particular the Natanson brothers; at their home he met, among others, Vallotton, Bonnard, and Vuillard, whose artistic experiments excited his admiration. He continued to work at a feverish pace, alternating paintings with posters, humorous drawings for newspapers and magazines, book illustrations, and color lithographs. But his heavy drinking was by then threatening his health and in 1899 his mother sent him to a clinic in Neuilly. Released from the clinic after three months, he relapsed into his former restless life. In July of 1901, after an attack of paralysis, he retired to live with his mother at the Château of Malromé, where he died on September 9.

Toulouse-Lautrec *Aristide Bruant in His Cabaret*, 1893, Paris, Bibliothèque Nationale, Cabinet des Estampes

HENRY VAN DE VELDE

Born at Antwerp in 1863. Studied painting in his native city and at Paris. He belonged to the group called "The Twenty" *(Les XX)* in Brussels, and in 1888 adopted the Divisionist technique of Seurat and Signac, taking part in the exhibit of the Independents in 1890. Shortly, however, disappointed in Seurat's attitude and theories, he left the Divisionist movement, even resolving to give up painting.

Van de Velde is better known as an architect than as a painter. A promoter of rational and functional architecture, he was one of the chief exponents of Art Nouveau. He was responsible for such buildings as the Folkwang Museum at Hagen (1902) and the Exposition Theater at Cologne (1914).

He died in Walchwil, on Lake Zurich, Switzerland, in 1957.

VINCENT VAN GOGH

Born March 30, 1853, at Groot-Zundert, in Holland. He was encouraged by his father, a Protestant pastor, to take up the career of an art dealer. From 1869 to 1873 he worked in the branch of the Goupil Gallery at The Hague, then (1873–75) in the London branch, and finally at the main gallery in Paris. A great lover of painting, he had, however, a profound lack of interest in the business of selling, and so at the beginning of 1876 he sud-

Toulouse-Lautrec *The Washerwoman*, 1888, Albi, Musée Toulouse-Lautrec

denly gave up his position. He was still uncertain what he wanted to do. At Ramsgate in England, he became a language teacher, then a lay preacher near London, and an apprentice bookseller at Dordrecht; he took courses in theology at Amsterdam and studied to be a missionary in Brussels. Finally, at the end of 1878, he was given the assignment of lay preacher in the mining region of the Borinage, in South Belgium, where he lived in the same misery and want as the miners.

But it was in the Borinage that he discovered painting as his vocation, after a profound self-examination in the summer of 1880, as revealed in a letter to his beloved brother, Theo. After leaving the Borinage, where he had filled his notebooks with sketches inspired by the life of the miners, van Gogh went first to Brussels to study anatomy and perspective, then to his family's new home at Etten, Holland. In December of 1881 he

His closest friendship was with Gauguin, whom he invited to join him at Arles after he retired there to work. Gauguin arrived on October 20, 1888, and the two months that followed were productive ones for both artists. But the difference in their temperaments and the continual arguments frayed van Gogh's nerves. The evening of December 24 he attacked Gauguin with a razor and a little later, frantic with remorse, cut off his own ear. It was the first of a series of violent seizures that tormented his last years.

In May of 1889 he entered the psychiatric hospital of Saint-Rémy and after a year transferred to Auvers-sur-Oise, where he put himself under the care of Dr. Gachet, a friend of Pissarro. For a time all seemed to go well, but after only two months, feeling the hopelessness of the recurrent and more frequent seizures, he shot himself, and died two days later, on July 29, 1890.

Van Gogh *Breton Women* (after a painting by E. Bernard), 1888, Milan, Galleria d'Arte Moderna, Grassi Collection

moved to The Hague, where, under the guidance of his cousin, Anton Mauve, he made his first serious efforts at painting. From 1883 to 1885 he lived and painted at Nuenen with his family; then, after studying at the Antwerp Academy (1885–86), he joined Theo in Paris. There he frequented Cormon's studio, where he met Toulouse-Lautrec and Anquetin, took part in the discussions inspired by the Impressionist crisis, sided with the Divisionists (led by Seurat) and Synthetists (Gauguin and his group), and met artists like Pissarro, Seurat, Signac, Bernard, and Gauguin.

THÉO VAN RYSSELBERGHE

Born in Ghent, Belgium, November 28, 1862. Completed his early art studies in his native city, then transferred to Brussels. Was one of the most active members of the group of artists called *Les XX*. In 1888 he joined the Divisionist movement, exhibiting thereafter at the shows of the Independents. He is remembered as an etcher and lithographer as well as a painter. Died at Saint-Clair, December 13, 1926.

List of Illustrations

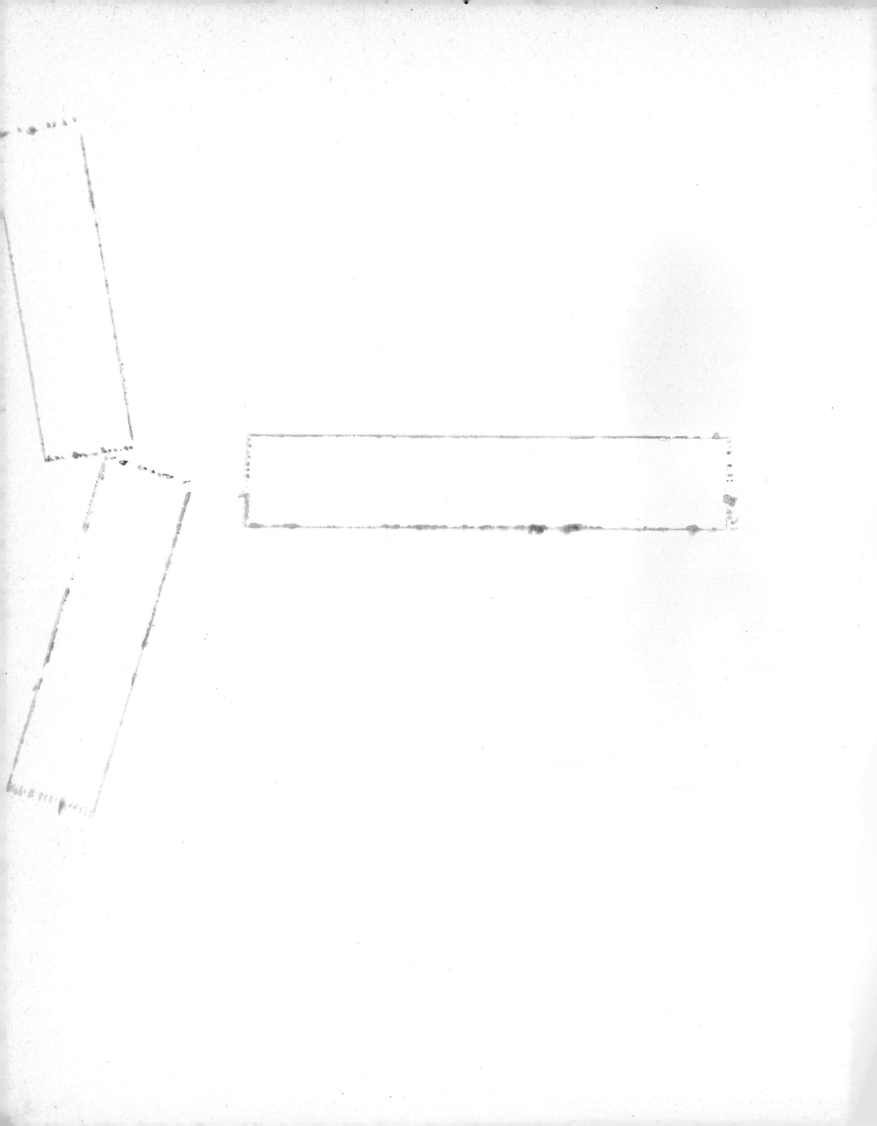